Tristan and I

Opera in Three A

Richard Wagner

Alpha Editions

This edition published in 2024

ISBN : 9789362097675

Design and Setting By
Alpha Editions
www.alphaedis.com
Email - info@alphaedis.com

As per information held with us this book is in Public Domain.
This book is a reproduction of an important historical work. Alpha Editions uses the best technology to reproduce historical work in the same manner it was first published to preserve its original nature. Any marks or number seen are left intentionally to preserve its true form.

THE STORY OF "TRISTAN AND ISOLDA"

ACT I

Tristan, a valiant Cornish knight, is bringing Isolda, princess of Ireland, over as a bride for his uncle, King Mark. He is himself in love with her, but owing to a blood feud between them, forces himself to conceal his passion. Isolda, in anger at his seeming unkindness, attempts to poison herself and him, but her attendant, Brangæna, changes the draft for a love potion, which enflames their passion beyond power of restraint.

ACT II

Isolda has been wedded to King Mark, but holds stolen interviews with Tristan, during one of which they are surprised, for Tristan has been betrayed by a jealous friend, Melot. Touched by King Mark's bitter reproaches, Tristan provokes Melot to fight and suffers himself to be mortally wounded.

ACT III

Tristan's faithful servant, Kurvenal, has carried his wounded master to his native home in Brittany, where he is carefully tended. Isolda has also been sent for, as being skilled above all others in the healing art. The excitement of her approach only hastens Tristan's death, and he breathes his last sigh in her arms. Mark has followed Isolda; he has had matters explained, and is prepared to reunite the lovers, but it is too late. Isolda utters her lament over the body of her lover, and her heart breaks: in death alone are they united.

DRAMATIS PERSONÆ		
TRISTAN		MELOT
KING MARK		BRANGÆNA
ISOLDA		A SHEPHERD
KURVENAL		A STEERSMAN
SAILORS, KNIGHTS, AND ESQUIRES		

TRISTAN AND ISOLDA.

ACT I.

[A pavilion erected on the deck of a ship, richly hung with tapestry, quite closed in at back at first. A narrow hatchway at one side leads below into the cabin.]

SCENE I.

ISOLDA *on a couch, her face buried in the cushions.*— BRANGÆNA *holding open a curtain, looks over the side of the vessel.*

THE VOICE OF A YOUNG SAILOR *(from above as if at the mast-head).*

ISOLDA *(starting up suddenly).*
What wight dares insult me?

(She looks round in agitation.)

Brangæna, ho!
Say, where sail we?

BRANGÆNA *(at the opening).*
Bluish stripes
are stretching along the west:
swiftly sails
the ship to shore;
if restful the sea by eve
we shall readily set foot on land.

ISOLDA. What land?

BRANGÆNA. Cornwall's verdant strand.

ISOLDA. Never more!
To-day nor to-morrow!

BRANGÆNA. What mean you, mistress? say!

(*She lets the curtain fall and hastens to* ISOLDA.)

ISOLDA (*with wild gaze*).
O fainthearted child,
false to thy fathers!
Ah, where, mother,
hast given thy might
that commands the wave and the tempest?
O subtle art
of sorcery,
for mere leech-craft followed too long!
Awake in me once more,
power of will!
Arise from thy hiding
within my breast!
Hark to my bidding,
fluttering breezes!
Arise and storm
in boisterous strife!
With furious rage
and hurricane's hurdle
waken the sea
from slumbering calm;
rouse up the deep
to its devilish deeds!
Shew it the prey
which gladly I proffer!
Let it shatter this too daring ship
and enshrine in ocean each shred!
And woe to the lives!
Their wavering death-sighs
I leave to ye, winds, as your lot.

BRANGÆNA (*in extreme alarm and concern for* ISOLDA).
Out, alas!
Ah, woe!
I've ever dreaded some ill!—
Isolda! mistress!
Heart of mine!
What secret dost thou hide?

Without a tear
thou'st quitted thy father and mother,
and scarce a word
of farewell to friends thou gavest;
leaving home thou stood'st,
how cold and still!
pale and speechless
on the way,
food rejecting,
reft of sleep,
stern and wretched,
wild, disturbed;
how it pains me
so to see thee!
Friends no more we seem,
being thus estranged.
Make me partner
in thy pain!
Tell me freely
all thy fears!
Lady, thou hearest,
sweetest and dearest;
if for true friend you take me,
your confidant O make me!

ISOLDA. Air! air!
or my heart will choke!
Open! open there wide!

(BRANGÆNA *hastily draws the centre curtains apart.*)

SCENE II.

[*The whole length of the ship is now seen, down to the stern, with the sea and horizon beyond. Round the mainmast sailors are ensconced, busied with ropes; beyond them in the stern are groups of knights and attendants, also seated; a little apart stands* TRISTAN *folding his arms and thoughtfully gazing out to sea; at his feet* KURVENAL *reclines carelessly. From the mast-head above is once more heard the voice of the young sailor.*]

THE YOUNG SAILOR (*at the mast-head invisible*).
The wind so wild
blows homewards now;
my Irish child,
where waitest thou?
Say, must our sails be weighted,

filled by thy sighs unbated?
Waft us, wind strong and wild!
Woe, ah woe for my child!

ISOLDA (*whose eyes have at once sought* TRISTAN *and fixed stonily on him—gloomily*). Once beloved—
now removed—
brave and bright,
coward knight!—
Death-devoted head!
Death-devoted heart!—

(*laughing unnaturally*).

Think'st highly of yon minion?

BRANGÆNA (*following her glance*).
Whom mean'st thou?

ISOLDA. There, that hero
who from mine eyes
averts his own:
in shrinking shame
my gaze he shuns—
Say, how hold you him?

BRANGÆNA. Mean you Sir Tristan,
lady mine?
Extolled by ev'ry nation,
his happy country's pride,
The hero of creation,—
whose fame so high and wide?

ISOLDA (*jeeringly*).
In shrinking trepidation
his shame he seeks to hide,
While to the king, his relation,
he brings the corpse-like bride!—
Seems it so senseless
What I say?
Go ask himself,
our gracious host,
dare he approach my side?
No courteous heed
or loyal care
this hero t'wards
his lady turns;

but to meet her his heart is daunted,
this knight so highly vaunted!
Oh! he wots
well the cause!
To the traitor go,
bearing his lady's will!
As my servant bound,
straightway should he approach.

BRANGÆNA. Shall I beseech him
to attend thee?

ISOLDA. Nay, order him:
pray, understand it:—
I, Isolda
do command it!

[*At an imperious sign from ISOLDA BRANGÆNA withdraws and timidly walks along the deck towards the stern, past the working sailors. ISOLDA, following her with fixed gaze, sinks back on the couch, where she remains seated during the following, her eyes still turned sternward.*]

KURVENAL (*observing Brangæna's approach, plucks Tristan by the robe without rising.*) Beware, Tristan!
Message from Isolda!

TRISTAN (*starting*). What is't?—Isolda?—

(*He quickly regains his composure as BRANGÆNA approaches and curtsies to him.*)

What would my lady?
I her liegeman,
fain will listen
while her loyal
woman tells her will.

BRANGÆNA. My lord, Sir Tristan,
Dame Isolda
would have speech
with you at once.

TRISTAN. Is she with travel worn?
The end is near:
nay, ere the set of sun
sight we the land.
All that your mistress commands me,
trust me, I shall mind.

BRANGÆNA. That you, Sir Tristan,
go to her,--
this is my lady's wish.

TRISTAN. Where yonder verdant meadows
in distance dim are mounting,
waits my sov'reign
for his mate:
to lead her to his presence
I'll wait upon the princess:
'tis an honor
all my own.

BRANGÆNA. My lord, Sir Tristan,
list to me:
this one thing
my lady wills,
that thou at once attend her,
there where she waits for thee.

TRISTAN. In any station
where I stand
I truly serve but her,
the pearl of womanhood.
If I unheeding
left the helm,
how might I pilot her ship
in surety to King Mark?

BRANGÆNA. Tristan, my master,
why mock me thus?
Seemeth my saying
obscure to you?
list to my lady's words:
thus, look you, she hath spoken:
"Go order him,
and understand it,
I—Isolda—
do command it."

KURVENAL (*springing up*). May I an answer make her?

TRISTAN. What wouldst thou wish to reply?

KURVENAL. This should she say
to Dame Isold':
"Though Cornwall's crown

and England's isle
for Ireland's child he chose,
his own by choice
she may not be;
he brings the king his bride.
A hero-knight
Tristan is hight!
I've said, nor care to measure
your lady's high displeasure."

[*While* TRISTAN *seeks to stop him, and the offended* BRANGÆNA *turns to depart,* KURVENAL *sings after her at the top of his voice, as she lingeringly withdraws.*]

"Sir Morold toiled
o'er mighty wave
the Cornish tax to levy;
In desert isle
was dug his grave,
he died of wounds so heavy.
His head now hangs
in Irish lands,
Sole were-gild won
at English hands.
Bravo, our brave Tristan!
Let his tax take who can!"

[KURVENAL, *driven away by* TRISTAN'S *chidings, descends into the cabin.* BRANGÆNA *returns in discomposure to* ISOLDA, *closing the curtains behind her, while all the men take up the chorus and are heard without.*]

KNIGHTS AND ATTENDANTS.
"His head now hangs
in Irish lands,
sole were-gild won
at English hands.
Bravo, our brave Tristan!
Let his tax take who can!"

SCENE III.

[ISOLDA *and* BRANGÆNA *alone, the curtain being again completely closed.* ISOLDA *rises with a gesture of despair and wrath.* BRANGÆNA *falls at her feet.*]

BRANGÆNA. Ah! an answer
so insulting!

ISOLDA (*checking herself on the brink of a fearful outburst*).
How now? of Tristan?
I'd know if he denies me.

BRANGÆNA. Ah! question not!

ISOLDA. Quick, say without fear!

BRANGÆNA. With courteous phrase
he foiled my will.

ISOLDA. But when you bade him hither?

BRANGÆNA. When I had straightway
bid him come,
where'er he stood,
he said to me,
he truly served but thee,
the pearl of womanhood;
if he unheeded
left the helm
how could he pilot the ship
in surety to King Mark?

ISOLDA (*bitterly*).
"How could he pilot the ship
in surety to King Mark!"
And wait on him with were-gild
from Ireland's island won!

BRANGÆNA.
As I gave out the message
and in thy very words,
thus spoke his henchman Kurvenal—

ISOLDA.
Heard I not ev'ry sentence?
it all has reached my ear.
If thou hast learnt my disgrace
now hear too whence it has grown.
How scoffingly
they sing about me!
Quickly could I requite them!
What of the boat
so bare and frail,
that floated by our shore?
What of the broken

stricken man,
feebly extended there?
Isolda's art
he gladly owned;
with herbs, simples
and healing salves
the wounds from which he suffered
she nursed in skilful wise.
Though "Tantris"
The name that he took unto him,
as "Tristan"
anon Isolda knew him,
when in the sick man's keen blade
she perceived a notch had been made,
wherein did fit
a splinter broken
in Morold's head,
the mangled token
sent home in hatred rare:
this hand did find it there.
I heard a voice
from distance dim;
with the sword in hand
I came to him.
Full well I willed to slay him,
for Morold's death to pay him.
But from his sick bed
he looked up
not at the sword,
not at my arm—
his eyes on mine were fastened,
and his feebleness
softened my heart:
the sword—dropped from my fingers.
Though Morold's steel had maimed him
to health again I reclaimed him!
when he hath homeward wended
my emotion then might be ended.

BRANGÆNA.
O wondrous! Why could I not see this?
The guest I sometime
helped to nurse—?

ISOLDA.
His praise briskly they sing now:—
"Bravo, our brave Tristan!"—
he was that distressful man.
A thousand protestations
of truth and love he prated.
Hear how a knight
fealty knows!—
When as Tantris
unforbidden he'd left me,
as Tristan
boldly back he came,
in stately ship
from which in pride
Ireland's heiress
in marriage he asked
for Mark, the Cornish monarch,
his kinsman worn and old.
In Morold's lifetime
dared any have dreamed
to offer us such an insult?
For the tax-paying
Cornish prince
to presume to court Ireland's princess!
Ah, woe is me!
I it was
who for myself
did shape this shame!
with death-dealing sword
should I have stabbed him;
weakly it escaped me:—
now serfdom I have shaped me.
Curse him, the villain!
Curse on his head!
Vengeance! Death!
Death for me too!

BRANGÆNA (*throwing herself upon* ISOLDA *with impetuous tenderness*).
Isolda! lady!
loved one! fairest!
sweet perfection!
mistress rarest!
Hear me! come now,
sit thee here.—

(*Gradually draws* ISOLDA *to the couch.*)

What a whim!
what causeless railing!
How came you so wrong-minded
and by mere fancy blinded?
Sir Tristan gives thee
Cornwall's kingdom;
then, were he erst thy debtor,
how could he reward thee better?
His noble uncle
serves he so:
think too what a gift
on thee he'd bestow!
With honor unequalled
all he's heir to
at thy feet he seeks to shower,
to make thee a queenly dower.

(ISOLDA *turns away.*)

If wife he'd make thee
unto King Mark
why wert thou in this wise complaining?
Is he not worth thy gaining?
Of royal race
and mild of mood,
who passes King Mark
in might and power?
If a noble knight
like Tristan serves him,
who would not but feel elated,
so fairly to be mated.

ISOLDA (*gazing vacantly before her*).
Glorious knight!
And I must near him
loveless ever languish!
How can I support such anguish?

BRANGÆNA.
What's this, my lady?
loveless thou?

(*Approaching coaxingly and kissing* ISOLDA.)

Where lives there a man
would not love thee?
Who could see Isolda
And not sink
at once into bondage blest?
And if e'en it could be
any were cold,
did any magic
draw him from thee,
I'd bring the false one
back to bondage,
And bind him in links of love.—

(*Secretly and confidentially, close to* ISOLDA.)

Mindest thou not
thy mother's arts?
Think you that she
who'd mastered those
would have sent me o'er the sea,
without assistance for thee?

ISOLDA (*darkly*).
My mother's rede
I mind aright,
and highly her magic
arts I hold:—
Vengeance they wreak for wrongs,
rest give to wounded spirits.—
Yon casket hither bear.

BRANGÆNA.
It holds a balm for thee.—

(*She brings forward a small golden coffer, opens it, and points to its contents.*)

Thy mother placed inside it
her subtle magic potions.
There's salve for sickness
or for wounds,
and antidotes
for deadly drugs.—

(*She takes a bottle.*)

The helpfullest draught
I hold in here.

ISOLDA.
Not so, I know a better.
I make a mark
to know it again—
This draught 'tis I would drain.

(*Seizes flask and shows it.*)

BRANGÆNA (*recoiling in horror*).
The draught of death!

(ISOLDA *has risen from the sofa and now hears with increasing dread the cries of the sailors.*)

VOICES OF THE CREW (*without*).
"Ho! heave ho! hey!
Reduce the sail!
The mainsail in!
Ho! heave ho! hey!"

ISOLDA.
Our journey has been swift.
Woe is me! Near to the land!

SCENE IV.

(KURVENAL *boisterously enters through the curtains.*)

KURVENAL.
Up, up, ye ladies!
Look alert!
Straight bestir you!
Loiter not,—here is the land!—
To dame Isolda
says the servant
of Tristan,
our hero true:—
Behold our flag is flying!
it waveth landwards aloft:
in Mark's ancestral castle
may our approach be seen.
So, dame Isolda,
he prays to hasten,
for land straight to prepare her,
that thither he may bear her.

ISOLDA (*who has at first cowered and shuddered on hearing the message, now speaks calmly and with dignity*). My greeting take
unto your lord
and tell him what I say now:
Should he assist to land me
and to King Mark would he hand me,
unmeet and unseemly
were his act,
the while my pardon
was not won
for trespass black and base:
So bid him seek my grace.

(KURVENAL *makes a gesture of defiance.*)

Now mark me well,
This message take:—
Nought will I yet prepare me,
that he to land may bear me;
I will not by him be landed,
nor unto King Mark be handed
ere granting forgiveness
and forgetfulness,
which 'tis seemly
he should seek:—
for all his trespass base
I tender him my grace.

KURVENAL.
Be assured,
I'll bear your words:
we'll see what he will say!

(*He retires quickly.*)

SCENE V.

ISOLDA (*hurries to* BRANGÆNA *and embraces her vehemently*).
Now farewell, Brangæna!
Greet ev'ry one,
Greet my father and mother!

BRANGÆNA.
What now? what mean'st thou?
Wouldst thou flee?
And where must I then follow?

ISOLDA (*checking herself suddenly*).
Here I remain:
heard you not?
Tristan will I await.—
I trust in thee
to aid in this:
prepare the true
cup of peace:
thou mindest how it is made.

BRANGÆNA.
What meanest thou?

ISOLDA (*taking a bottle from the coffer*).
This it is!
From the flask go pour
this philtre out;
yon golden goblet 'twill fill.

BRANGÆNA (*filled with terror receiving the flask*).
Trust I my wits?

ISOLDA.
Wilt thou be true?

BRANGÆNA.
The draught—for whom?

ISOLDA. Him who betrayed!

BRANGÆNA. Tristan?

ISOLDA. Truce he'll drink with me.

BRANGÆNA (*throwing herself at* ISOLDA'S *feet*). O horror!
Pity thy handmaid!

ISOLDA. Pity thou me,
false-hearted maid!
Mindest thou not
my mother's arts?
Think you that she
who'd mastered those
would have sent thee o'er the sea
without assistance for me?
A salve for sickness
doth she offer
and antidotes

for deadly drugs:
for deepest grief
and woe supreme
gave she the draught of death.
Let Death now give her thanks!

BRANGÆNA (*scarcely able to control herself*). O deepest grief!

ISOLDA. Now, wilt thou obey?

BRANGÆNA. O woe supreme!

ISOLDA. Wilt thou be true?

BRANGÆNA. The draught?

KURVENAL (*entering*). Sir Tristan!

(BRANGÆNA *rises, terrified and confused.* ISOLDA *strives with immense effort to control herself.*)

ISOLDA (*to Kurvenal*). Sir Tristan may approach!

SCENE VI.

[KURVENAL *retires again.* BRANGÆNA, *almost beside herself, turns up the stage.* ISOLDA, *mustering all her powers of resolution, walks slowly and with dignity towards the sofa, by the head of which she supports herself, turning her eyes firmly towards the entrance*]

(TRISTAN *enters, and pauses respectfully at the entrance.*)

TRISTAN. Demand, lady,
what you will.

ISOLDA. While knowing not
what my demand is,
wert thou afraid
still to fulfil it,
fleeing my presence thus?

TRISTAN. Honor
Held me in awe.

ISOLDA. Scant honor hast thou
shown unto me;
for, unabashed,
withheldest thou
obedience unto my call.

TRISTAN. Obedience 'twas
forbade me to come.

ISOLDA. But little I owe
thy lord, methinks,
if he allows
ill manners
unto his own promised bride.

TRISTAN. In our land
it is the law
that he who fetches
home the bride
should stay afar from her.

ISOLDA. On what account?

TRISTAN. 'Tis the custom.

ISOLDA. Being so careful,
my lord Tristan,
another custom
can you not learn?
Of enemies friends make:
for evil acts amends make.

TRISTAN. Who is my foe?

ISOLDA. Find in thy fears!
Blood-guilt
gets between us.

TRISTAN. That was absolved.

ISOLDA. Not between us.

TRISTAN. In open field,
'fore all the folk
our old feud was abandoned.

ISOLDA. 'Twas not there
I held Tantris hid
when Tristan was laid low,

He stood there brawny,
bright and brave;
but in his truce
I took no part:
my tongue its silence had learnt.
When in chambered stillness
sick he lay
with the sword I stood
before him, stern;
silent—my lips,
motionless—my hand.
But that which my hand
and lips had once vowed,
I swore in stealth to adhere to:
lo! now my desire I'm near to.

TRISTAN. What hast thou sworn?

ISOLDA (*quickly*). Vengeance for Morold!

TRISTAN (*quietly*). Mindst thou that?

ISOLDA (*animated*). Dare you to flout me?—
Was he not my betrothed,
that noble Irish knight?
For his sword a blessing I sought;
for me only he fought.
When he was murdered
no honor fell.
In that heartfelt misery
my vow was framed;
if no man remained to right it,
I, a maid, must needs requite it.—
Weak and maimed,
when might was mine,
why at thy death did I pause?
Thou shalt know the secret cause.—
Thy hurts I tended
that, when sickness ended,
thou shouldst fall by some man,
as Isolda's revenge should plan.
But now attempt
thy fate to foretell me?
if their friendship all men do sell thee,
what foe can seek to fell thee?

TRISTAN (*pale and gloomy, offers her his sword*). If
thou so lovedst this lord,
then lift once more my sword,
nor from thy purpose refrain;
let the weapon not fail again.

ISOLDA. Put up thy sword
which once I swung,
when vengeful rancor
my bosom wrung,
when thy masterful eyes
did ask me straight
whether King Mark
might seek me for mate.
The sword harmless descended.—
Drink, let our strife be ended!

(ISOLDA *beckons* BRANGÆNA. *She trembles and hesitates to obey.* ISOLDA *commands her with a more imperious gesture.* BRANGÆNA *sets about preparing the drink.*)

VOICES OF THE CREW (*without*). Ho! heave ho! hey!
Reduce the sail!
The foresail in!
Ho! heave ho! hey!

TRISTAN (*starting from his gloomy brooding*). Where
are we?

ISOLDA. Near to shore.
Tristan, is warfare ended?
Hast not a word to offer?

TRISTAN (*darkly*). Concealment's mistress
makes me silent:
I know what she conceals,
conceal, too, more than she knows.

ISOLDA. Thy silence nought
but feigning I deem.
Friendship wilt thou still deny?

(*Renewed cries of the Sailors.*)

(*At an impatient sign from* ISOLDA BRANGÆNA *hands her the filled cup.*)

ISOLDA (*advancing with the cup to* TRISTAN, *who gazes immovably into her eyes*).
Thou hear'st the cry?

The shore's in sight:
we must ere long (*with slight scorn*)
stand by King Mark together.

SAILORS (*without*). Haul the warp!
Anchor down!

TRISTAN (*starting wildly*). Down with the anchor!
Her stern to the stream!
The sails a-weather the mast!

(*He takes the cup from* ISOLDA.)

I know the Queen
of Ireland well,
unquestioned are
her magic arts:
the balsam cured me
which she brought;
now bid me quaff the cup,
that I may quite recover.
Heed to my all—
atoning oath,
which in return I tender
Tristan's honor—
highest truth!
Tristan's anguish—
brave distress!
Traitor spirit,
dawn-illumined!
Endless trouble's
only truce!
Oblivion's kindly draught,
with rapture thou art quaff'd!

(*He lifts the cup and drinks.*)

ISOLDA. Betrayed e'en here?
I must halve it!—

(*She wrests the cup from his hand.*)

Betrayer, I drink to thee!

[*She drinks, and then throws away the cup. Both, seized with shuddering, gaze with deepest emotion, but immovable demeanor, into one another's eyes, in which the expression of defiance to death fades and melts into the glow of passion. Trembling seizes them, they* convulsively clutch their hearts and pass their hands over their brows. Their glances again seek to meet, sink in confusion, and once more turn with growing longing upon one another.]

ISOLDA (*with trembling voice*). Tristan!

TRISTAN (*overpowered*). Isolda!

ISOLDA (*sinking upon his breast*). Traitor beloved!

TRISTAN. Woman divine!

(*He embraces her with ardor. They remain in a silent embrace.*)

ALL THE MEN (*without*). Hail! Hail!
Hail our monarch!
Hail to Mark, the king!

BRANGÆNA (*who, filled with confusion and horror, has leaned over the side with averted face, now turns to behold the pair locked in their close embrace, and rushes to the front, wringing her hands in despair*). Woe's me! Woe's me!
Endless mis'ry
I have wrought
instead of death!
Dire the deed
of my dull fond heart:
it cries aloud to heav'n!

(*They start from their embrace.*)

TRISTAN (*bewildered*). What troubled dream
of Tristan's honor?

ISOLDA. What troubled dream
Of Isolda's shame?

TRISTAN. Have I then lost thee?

ISOLDA. Have I repulsed thee?

TRISTAN. Fraudulent magic,
framing deceit!

BOTH. Languishing passion,
longing and growing,
love ever yearning,
loftiest glowing!
Rapture confess'd
rides in each breast!
Isolda! Tristan!
Tristan! Isolda!

World, I can shun thee
my love is won me!
Thou'rt my thought, all above:
highest delight of love!

SCENE VII.

[*The curtains are now drawn wide apart; the whole ship is covered with knights and sailors, who, with shouts of joy, make signs over towards the shore which is now seen to be quite near, with castle-crowned cliffs. Tristan and Isolda remain absorbed in mutual contemplation, perceiving nothing that is passing.*]

BRANGÆNA (*to the women, who at her bidding ascend from below*).
Quick—the mantle!
the royal robe!—

(*Rushing between* TRISTAN *and* ISOLDA.)

Up, hapless ones!
See where we are!

(*She places the royal mantle on* ISOLDA, *who notices nothing.*)

ALL THE MEN. Hail! Hail!
Hail our monarch!
Hail to Mark the king!

KURVENAL (*advancing gaily*). Hail, Tristan,
knight of good hap!
Behold King Mark approaching,
in a bark
with brave attendance.
Gladly he stems the tide,
coming to seek his bride.

TRISTAN (*looking up in bewilderment*). Who comes?

KURVENAL. The king 'tis.

TRISTAN. What king mean you?

(KURVENAL *points over the side.* TRISTAN *gazes stupefied at the shore.*)

ALL THE MEN (*waving their hats*). Hail to King Mark!
All hail!

ISOLDA (*bewildered*). What is't, Brangæna?
What are those cries?

BRANGÆNA. Isolda—mistress!
Compose thyself!

ISOLDA. Where am I! living?
What was that draught?

BRANGÆNA (*despairingly*). The love-potion!

ISOLDA (*staring with horror at* TRISTAN). Tristan!

TRISTAN. Isolda!

ISOLDA. Must I live, then?

(*Falls fainting upon his breast.*)

BRANGÆNA (*to the women*). Look to your lady!

TRISTAN. O rapture fraught with cunning!
O fraud with bliss o'er-running!

ALL THE MEN (*in a general burst of acclamation*).
Hail to King Mark!
Cornwall, hail!

[*People have clambered over the ship's side, others have extended a bridge, and the aspect of all indicates the immediate arrival of the expected ones, as the curtain falls.*]

ACT II.

[*A Garden before* ISOLDA'S *Chamber which lies at one side and is approached by steps. Bright and pleasant summer night. At the open door a burning torch is fixed. Sounds of hunting heard.*]

SCENE I.

[BRANGÆNA, *on the steps leading to the chamber, is watching the retreat of the still audible hunters. She looks anxiously back into the chamber as* ISOLDA *emerges thence in ardent animation.*]

ISOLDA. Yet do you hear?
I lost the sound some time.

BRANGÆNA (*listening*). Still do they stay:
clearly rings the horns.

ISOLDA (*listening*). Fear but deludes
thy anxious ear;
by sounds of rustling

leaves thou'rt deceived,
aroused by laughter of winds.

BRANGÆNA. Deceived by wild
desire art thou,
and but hear'st as would thy will:—
I still hear the sound of horns.

ISOLDA (*listens*). No sound of horns
were so sweet:
yon fountain's soft
murmuring current
moves so quietly hence.
If horns yet brayed,
how could I hear that?
In still night alone
it laughs on mine ear.
My lov'd one hides
in darkness unseen:
wouldst thou hold from my side my dearest?
deeming that horns thou hearest?

BRANGÆNA. Thy lov'd one hid—
oh heed my warning!—
for him a spy waits by night.
Listening oft
I light upon him:
he lays a secret snare.
Of Melot oh beware!

ISOLDA. Mean you Sir Melot?
O, how you mistake!
Is he not Tristan's
trustiest friend?
May my true love not meet me,
with none but Melot he stays.

BRANGÆNA. What moves me to fear him
makes thee his friend then?
Through Tristan to Mark's side
is Melot's way:
he sows suspicion's seed.
And those who have
to-day on a night-hunt
so suddenly decided,
a far nobler game

than is guessed by thee
taxes their hunting skill.

ISOLDA. For Tristan's sake
contrived was this scheme
by means of
Melot, in truth:
now would you decry his friendship?
He serves Isolda
better than you
his hand gives help
which yours denies:
what need of such delay?
The signal, Brangæna!
O give the signal!
Tread out the torch's
trembling gleam,
that night may envelop
all with her veil.
Already her peace reigns
o'er hill and hall,
her rapturous awe
the heart does enthral;
allow then the light to fall!
Let but its dread lustre die!
let my beloved draw nigh!

BRANGÆNA. The light of warning suppress not!
Let it remind thee of peril!—
Ah, woe's me! Woe's me!
Fatal folly!
The fell pow'r of that potion!
That I framed
a fraud for once
thy orders to oppose!
Had I been deaf and blind,
thy work
were then thy death:
but thy distress,
thy distraction of grief,
my work
has contrived them, I own it!

ISOLDA. Thy—act?
O foolish girl!

Love's goddess dost thou not know?
nor all her magic arts?
The queen who grants
unquailing hearts,
the witch whose will
the world obeys,
life and death
she holds in her hands,
which of joy and woe are wove?
she worketh hate into love.
The work of death
I took into my own hands;
Love's goddess saw
and gave her good commands
The death—condemned
she claimed as her prey,
planning our fate
in her own way.
How she may bend it,
how she may end it,
what she may make me,
wheresoe'er take me,
still hers am I solely;—
so let me obey her wholly.

BRANGÆNA. And if by the artful
love-potion's lures
thy light of reason is ravished,
if thou art reckless
when I would warn thee,
this once, oh, wait
and weigh my pleading!
I implore, leave it alight!—
The torch! the torch!
O put it not out this night!

ISOLDA. She who causes thus
my bosom's throes,
whose eager fire
within me glows,
whose light upon
my spirit flows,
Love's goddess needs
that night should close;

that brightly she may reign
and shun the torchlight vain.

(*She goes up to the door and takes down the torch.*)

Go watch without—
keep wary guard!
The signal!—
and were it my spirit's spark,
smiling
I'd destroy it and hail the dark!

[*She throws the torch to the ground where it slowly dies out. BRANGÆNA turns away, disturbed, and mounts an outer flight of steps leading to the roof, where she slowly disappears. ISOLDA listens and peers, at first shyly, towards an avenue. Urged, by rising impatience, she then approaches the avenue and looks more boldly. She signs with her handkerchief, first slightly, then more plainly, waving it quicker as her impatience increases. A gesture of sudden delight shows that she has perceived her lover in the distance. She stretches herself higher and higher, and then, to look better over the intervening space, hastens back to the steps, from the top of which she signals again to the on-comer. As he enters, she springs to meet him.*]

SCENE II.

TRISTAN (*rushing in*). Isolda! Beloved!

ISOLDA. Tristan! Beloved one!

(*Passionate embrace, with which they come down to the front.*)

BOTH. Art thou mine?
Do I behold thee?
Do I embrace thee?
Can I believe it?
At last! At last!
Here on my breast!
Do I then clasp thee!
Is it thy own self?
Are these thine eyes?
These thy lips?
Here thy hand?
Here thy heart?
Is't I?—Is't thou,
held in my arms?
Am I not duped?
Is it no dream?
O rapture of spirit!

O sweetest, highest,
fairest, strongest,
holiest bliss?
Endless pleasure!
Boundless treasure!
Ne'er to sever!
Never! Never!
Unconceived,
unbelieved,
overpowering
exaltation!
Joy-proclaiming,
bliss-outpouring,
high in heaven,
earth ignoring!
Tristan mine!
Isolda mine!
Tristan!
Isolda!
Mine alone!
Thine alone!
Ever all my own!

TRISTAN. The light! The light!
O but this light,
how long 'twas let to burn!
The sun had sunk,
the day had fled;
but all their spite
not yet was sped:
the scaring signal
they set alight,
before my belov'd one's dwelling,
my swift approach repelling.

ISOLDA. Thy belov'd one's hand
lowered the light,
for Brangæna's fears
in me roused no fright:
while Love's goddess gave me aid,
sunlight a mock I made.
But the light its fear
and defeat repaid;
with thy misdeeds

a league it made.
What thou didst see
in shadowing night,
to the shining sun
of kingly might
must thou straightway surrender,
that it should
exist in bright
bonds of empty splendor.—
Could I bear it then?
Can I bear it now?

TRISTAN. O now were we
to night devoted,
the dishonest day
with envy bloated,
lying, could not mislead,
though it might part us indeed.
Its pretentious glows
and its glamouring light
are scouted by those
who worship night.
All its flickering gleams
in flashes out-blazing
blind us no more
where we are gazing.
Those who death's night
boldly survey,
those who have studied
her secret way,
the daylight's falsehoods—
rank and fame,
honor and all
at which men aim—
to them are no more matter
than dust which sunbeams scatter,
In the daylight's visions thronging
only abides one longing;
we yearn to hie
to holy night,
where, unending,
only true,
Love extendeth delight!

(TRISTAN draws ISOLDA gently aside to a flowery bank, sinks on his knee before her and rests his head on her arm.)

(TRISTAN *and* ISOLDA *sink into oblivious ecstasy, reposing on the flowery bank close together.*)

BRANGÆNA *(from the turret, unseen)*. Long I watch
alone by night:
ye enwrapt
in love's delight,
heed my boding
voice aright.
I forewarn you
woe is near;
waken to
my words of fear.
Have a care!
Have a care!
Swiftly night doth wear!

ISOLDA. List, beloved!

TRISTAN. Let me die thus!

ISOLDA *(slowly raising herself a little)*. Envious
watcher!

TRISTAN *(remaining in reclining position)*. I'll ne'er
waken.

ISOLDA. But the Day
must dawn and rouse thee?

TRISTAN (*raising his head slightly*). Let the Day
to Death surrender!

ISOLDA. Day and Death
will both engender
feud against
our passion tender.

TRISTAN (*drawing* ISOLDA *gently towards him with expressive action*). O might
we then
together die,
each the other's
own for aye!
never fearing,
never waking,
blest delights
of love partaking,—
each to each be given,
in love alone our heaven!

ISOLDA (*gazing up at him in thoughtful ecstasy*).
O might we then
together die!

TRISTAN. Each the other's—

ISOLDA. Own for aye,—

TRISTAN. Never fearing—

ISOLDA. Never waking—

TRISTAN. Blest delights
of love partaking—

ISOLDA. Each to each be given;
in love alone our heaven.

(ISOLDA, *as if overcome, droops her head on his breast.*)

BRANGÆNA'S VOICE (*as before*).
Have a care!
Have a care!
Night yields to daylight's glare.

TRISTAN (*bends smilingly to* ISOLDA).
Shall I listen?

ISOLDA (looking fondly up at TRISTAN).
Let me die thus!

TRISTAN. Must I waken?

ISOLDA. Nought shall wake me!

TRISTAN. Must not daylight
dawn, and rouse me?

ISOLDA. Let the Day
to Death surrender!

TRISTAN. May thus the Day's
evil threats be defied?

ISOLDA (*with growing enthusiasm*).
From its thraldom let us fly.

TRISTAN. And shall not its dawn
be dreaded by us?

ISOLDA (*rising with a grand gesture*).
Night will shield us for aye!

(TRISTAN *follows her; they embrace in fond exaltation.*)

BOTH. O endless Night!
blissful Night!
glad and glorious
lover's Night!
Those whom thou holdest,
lapped in delight,
how could e'en the boldest
unmoved endure thy flight?
How to take it,
how to break it,—
joy existent,
sunlight distant,
Far from mourning,
sorrow-warning,
fancies spurning,
softly yearning,
fear expiring,
sweet desiring!
Anguish flying,
gladly dying;
no more pining,
night-enshrining,
ne'er divided
whate'er betided,

side by side
still abide
in realms of space unmeasured,
vision blest and treasured!
Thou Isolda,
Tristan I;
no more Tristan,
no more Isolda.
Never spoken,
never broken,
newly sighted,
newly lighted,
endless ever
all our dream:
in our bosoms gleam
love delights supreme!

SCENE III.

[BRANGÆNA *utters a piercing cry.* TRISTAN *and* ISOLDA *remain in their absorbed state.* KURVENAL *rushes in with drawn sword.*]

KURVENAL. Save yourself, Tristan!

[*He looks fearfully off behind him.* MARK, MELOT, *and courtiers, in hunting dress, come swiftly up the avenue and pause in the foreground in consternation before the lovers.* BRANGÆNA *at the same time descends from the roof and hastens towards* ISOLDA. *The latter in involuntary shame leans on the flowery bank with averted face.* TRISTAN *with an equally unconscious action stretches his mantle wide out with one arm, so as to conceal* ISOLDA *from the gaze of the new-comers. In this position he remains for some time, turning a changeless look upon the men, who gaze at him in varied emotion. The morning dawns.*]

TRISTAN. The dreary day—
its last time comes!

MELOT (*to Mark*). Now say to me, my sov'reign,
was my impeachment just?
I staked my head thereon:
How is the pledge redeemed?
Behold him in
the very act:
honor and fame,
faithfully I
have saved from shame for thee.

MARK (*deeply moved, with trembling voice*). Hast thou
preserved them?
Say'st thou so?—
See him there,
the truest of all true hearts!
Look on him
the faithfulest of friends, too
His offence
so black and base
fills my heart
with anguish and disgrace.
Tristan traitor,
what hope stayeth
that the honor
he betrayeth
should by Melot's rede
rest to me indeed?

TRISTAN (*with convulsive violence*). Daylight phantoms—
morning visions
empty and vain—
Avaunt! Begone!

MARK (*in deep emotion*). This—blow.
Tristan, to me?
Where now has truth fled,
if Tristan can betray?
Where now are faith
and friendship fair,
when from the fount of faith,
my Tristan, they are gone?
The buckler Tristan
once did don,
where is that shield
of virtue now?
when from my friends it flies,
and Tristan's honor dies?

(TRISTAN *slowly lowers his eyes to the ground. His features express increasing grief while* MARK *continues.*)

Why hast thou noble
service done,
and honor, fame
and potent might

amassed for Mark, thy king?
Must honor, fame,
power and might,
must all thy noble
service done
be paid with Mark's dishonor?
Seemed the reward
too slight and scant
that what thou hast won him—
realms and riches—
thou art the heir unto, all?
When childless he lost
once a wife,
he loved thee so
that ne'er again
did Mark desire to marry.
When all his subjects,
high and low,
demands and pray'rs,
on him did press
to choose himself a consort—
a queen to give the kingdom,
when thou thyself
thy uncle urged
that what the court
and country pleaded
well might be conceded,
opposing high and low,
opposing e'en thyself,
with kindly cunning
still he refused,
till, Tristan, thou didst threaten
forever to leave
both court and land
if thou receivedst
not command
a bride for the king to woo:
then so he let thee do.—
This wondrous lovely wife,
thy might for me did win,
who could behold her,
who address her,
who in pride

and bliss possess her,
but would bless his happy fortune?
She whom I have
paid respect to ever,
whom I owned,
yet possess'd her never
she, the princess
proud and peerless,
lighting up
my life so cheerless,
'spite foes,—without fear,
the fairest of brides
thou didst bring me here.
Why in hell must I bide,
without hope of a heaven?
Why endure disgrace
unhealed by tears or grief?
The unexplained,
unpenetrated
cause of all these woes,
who will to us disclose?

TRISTAN (*raising his eyes pitifully towards* MARK).
O monarch! I—
may not tell thee, truly;
what thou dost ask
remains for aye unanswered.—

(*He turns to* ISOLDA, *who looks tenderly up at him.*)

Where Tristan now is going,
wilt thou, Isolda, follow?
The land that Tristan means
of sunlight has no gleams;
it is the dark
abode of night,
from whence I first
came forth to light,
and she who bore me
thence in anguish,
gave up her life,
nor long did languish.
She but looked on my face,
then sought this resting-place.
This land where Night doth reign,

where Tristan once hath lain—
now thither offers he
thy faithful guide to be.
So let Isolda
straight declare
if she will meet him there.

ISOLDA. When to a foreign land
before thou didst invite,
to thee, traitor,
resting true,
did Isolda follow.
Thy kingdom now art showing,
where surely we are going!
why should I shun that land
by which the world is spann'd?
For Tristan's house and home
Isold' will make her own.
The road whereby
we have to go
I pray thee quickly show!—

(TRISTAN *bends slowly over her and kisses her softly on the forehead.* MELOT *starts furiously forward.*)

MELOT (*drawing his sword*). Thou villain! Ha!
Avenge thee, monarch!
Say, wilt suffer such scorn?

TRISTAN (*drawing his sword and turning quickly round*)
Who's he will set his life against mine?

(*casting a look at* MELOT).

This was my friend;
he told me he loved me truly:
my fame and honor
he upheld more than all men.
With arrogance
he filled my heart,
and led on those
who prompted me
fame and pow'r to augment me
by wedding thee to our monarch.—
Thy glance, Isolda,
glamoured him thus;

and, jealous, my friend
played me false
to King Mark, whom I betrayed.—

(*He sets on* MELOT.)

Guard thee, Melot!

[*As* MELOT *presents his sword* TRISTAN *drops his own guard and sinks wounded into the arms of* KURVENAL. ISOLDA *throws herself upon his breast.* MARK *holds* MELOT *back. The curtain falls quickly.*]

ACT III.

A Castle-Garden.

[*At one side high castellated buildings, on the other a low breastwork interrupted by a watch tower; at back the castle-gate. The situation is supposed to be on rocky cliffs; through openings the view extends over a wide sea horizon. The whole gives an impression of being deserted by the owner, badly kept, and here and there dilapidated and overgrown.*]

SCENE I.

[*In the foreground, in the garden, lies* TRISTAN *sleeping on a couch under the shade of a great lime-tree, stretched out as if lifeless. At his head sits* KURVENAL, *bending over him in grief and anxiously listening to his breathing. From without comes the mournful sound of a shepherd's pipe.*

Presently the shepherd comes and looks in with interest, showing the upper half of his body over the wall.]

SHEPHERD. Kurvenal, ho!—
Say, Kurvenal,—
tell me, friend!
Does he still sleep?

KURVENAL (turning a little towards him and shaking his head sadly). If he awoke
it would be
but for evermore to leave us,
unless we find
the lady-leech;
alone can she give help.—
See'st thou nought?
No ship yet on the sea?

SHEPHERD. Quite another ditty
then would I play

as merry as ever I may.
But tell me truly,
trusty friend,
why languishes our lord?

KURVENAL. Do not ask me;—
for I can give no answer.
Watch the sea,
if sails come in sight
a sprightly melody play.

SHEPHERD (*turns round and scans the horizon, shading his eyes with his hand*).
Blank appears the sea!

(*He puts the reed pipe to his mouth and withdraws, playing.*)

TRISTAN (*motionless—faintly*).
The tune so well known—
why wake to that?

(*opens his eyes and slightly turns his head*).

Where am I?

KURVENAL (*starting in joyous surprise*).
Ha!—who is speaking?
It is his voice!—
Tristan! lov'd one!
My lord! my Tristan!

TRISTAN (*with effort*). Who—calls me?

KURVENAL. Life—at last—
O thanks be to heaven!—
sweetest life
unto my Tristan newly given!

TRISTAN (*faintly*). Kurvenal!—thou?
Where—was I?—
Where—am I?

KURVENAL. Where art thou?
In safety, tranquil and sure!
Kareol 'tis;
dost thou not know
thy fathers' halls?

TRISTAN. This my fathers'?

KURVENAL. Look but around.

TRISTAN. What awoke me?

KURVENAL. The herdsman's ditty
hast thou heard, doubtless;
he heedeth thy herds
above on the hills there.

TRISTAN. Have I herds, then?

KURVENAL. Sir, I say it!
Thine are court,
castle—all.
To thee yet true,
thy trusty folk,
as best they might,
have held thy home in guard:
the gift which once
thy goodness gave
to thy serfs and vassals here,
when going far away,
in foreign lands to dwell.

TRISTAN. What foreign land?

KURVENAL. Why! in Cornwall;
where cool and able,
all that was brilliant,
brave and noble,
Tristan, my lord, lightly took.

TRISTAN. Am I in Cornwall?

KURVENAL. No, no; in Kareol.

TRISTAN. How came I here?

KURVENAL. Hey now! how you came?
No horse hither you rode:
a vessel bore you across.
But on my shoulders
down to the ship
you had to ride: they are broad,
they carried you to the shore.
Now you are at home once more;
your own the land,
your native land;
all loved things now are near you,
unchanged the sun doth cheer you.

The wounds from which you languish
here all shall end their anguish.

(*He presses himself to* TRISTAN'S *breast.*)

TRISTAN. Think'st thou thus!
I know 'tis not so,
but this I cannot tell thee.
Where I awoke
ne'er I was,
but where I wandered
I can indeed not tell thee.
The sun I could not see,
nor country fair, nor people;
but what I saw
I can indeed not tell thee.
It was—
the land from which I once came
and whither I return:
the endless realm
of earthly night.
One thing only
there possessed me:
blank, unending,
all-oblivion.—
How faded all forebodings!
O wistful goadings!—
Thus I call
the thoughts that all
t'ward light of day have press'd me.
What only yet doth rest me,
the love-pains that possess'd me,
from blissful death's affright
now drive me toward the light,
which, deceitful, bright and golden,
round thee, Isolda, shines.
Accursèd day
with cruel glow!
Must thou ever
wake my woe?
Must thy light
be burning ever,
e'en by night
our hearts to sever?

Ah, my fairest,
sweetest, rarest!
When wilt thou—
when, ah, when—
let the torchlight dwindle,
that so my bliss may kindle?
The light, how long it glows!
When will the house repose?

(His voice has grown fainter and he sinks back gently, exhausted.)

KURVENAL *(who has been deeply distressed, now quickly rousts himself from his dejection)*.
I once defied,
through faith in thee,
the one for whom
now with thee I'm yearning.
Trust in my words,
thou soon shalt see her
face to face.
My tongue that comfort giveth,—
if on the earth still she liveth.

TRISTAN *(very feebly)*. Yet burns the beacon's spark:
yet is the house not dark,
Isolda lives and wakes:
her voice through darkness breaks.

KURVENAL. Lives she still,
then let new hope delight thee.
If foolish and dull you hold me,
this day you must not scold me.
As dead lay'st thou
since the day
when that accursed Melot
so foully wounded thee.
Thy wound was heavy:
how to heal it?
Thy simple servant
there bethought
that she who once
closed Morold's wound
with ease the hurt could heal thee
that Melot's sword did deal thee.
I found the best

of leeches there,
to Cornwall have I
sent for her:
a trusty serf
sails o'er the sea,
bringing Isold' to thee.

TRISTAN (*transported*). Isolda comes!
Isolda nears! (He struggles for words.)
O friendship! high
and holy friendship!

(*Draws* KURVENAL *to him and embraces him.*)

O Kurvenal,
thou trusty heart,
my truest friend I rank thee!
Howe'er can Tristan thank thee?
My shelter and shield
in fight and strife;
in weal or woe
thou'rt mine for life.
Those whom I hate
thou hatest too;
those whom I love
thou lovest too.
When good King Mark
I followed of old,
thou wert to him truer than gold.
When I was false
to my noble friend,
to betray too thou didst descend.
Thou art selfless,
solely mine;
thou feel'st for me
when I suffer.
But—what I suffer,
thou canst not feel for me!
this terrible yearning in my heart,
this feverish burning's
cruel smart,—
did I but show it,
couldst thou but know it,
no time here wouldst thou tarry,
to watch from tow'r thou wouldst hurry;

with all devotion
viewing the ocean,
with eyes impatiently spying,
there, where her ship's sails are flying.
Before the wind she
drives to find me;
on the wings of love she neareth,—
Isolda hither steereth!—
she nears, she nears,
so boldly and fast!
It waves, it waves,
the flag from the mast!
Hurra! Hurra!
she reaches the bar!
Dost thou not see?
Kurvenal, dost thou not see?

(*As* KURNEVAL *hesitates to leave* TRISTAN, *who is gazing at him in mute expectation, the mournful tune of the shepherd is heard, as before.*)

KURVENAL (*dejectedly*). Still is no ship in sight.

TRISTAN (*has listened with waning excitement and now recommences with growing melancholy*).
Is this the meaning then,
thou old pathetic ditty,
of all thy sighing sound?—
On evening's breeze
it sadly rang
when, as a child,
my father's death-news chill'd me;
through morning's mist
it stole more sadly,
when the son
his mother's fate was taught,
when they who gave me breath
both felt the hand of death
to them came also
through their pain
the ancient ditty's
yearning strain,
which asked me once
and asks me now
which was the fate before me
to which my mother bore me?—

What was the fate?—
The strain so plaintive
now repeats it:—
for yearning—and dying!

(*He falls back senseless.*)

KURVENAL (*who has been vainly striving to calm* TRISTAN, *cries out in terror*).
My master! Tristan!—
Frightful enchantment!—
O love's deceit!
O passion's pow'r!
Most sweet dream 'neath the sun,
see the work thou hast done!—
Here lies he now,
the noblest of knights,
with his passion all others above:
behold! what reward
his ardor requites;
the one sure reward of love!

(*with sobbing voice.*)

Art thou then dead?
Liv'st thou not?
Hast to the curse succumbed?—

(*He listens for* TRISTAN'S *breath.*)

O rapture! No!
He still moves! He lives!
and gently his lips are stirr'd.

TRISTAN (*very faintly*). The ship—is't yet in sight?

KURVENAL. The ship? Be sure
t'will come to-day:
it cannot tarry longer.

TRISTAN. On board Isolda,—
see, she smiles—
with the cup
that reconciles.
Dost thou see?
Dost thou see her now?
Full of grace
and loving mildness,
floating o'er

the ocean's wildness?
By billows of flowers
lightly lifted,
gently toward
the land she's drifted.
Her look brings ease
and sweet repose;
her hand one last
relief bestows.
Isolda! Ah, Isolda!
How fair, how sweet art thou!—
And Kurvenal, why!—
what ails thy sight?
Away, and watch for her,
foolish I see so well and plainly,
let not thine eye seek vainly
Dost thou not hear?
Away, with speed!
Haste to the watch-tow'r!
Wilt thou not heed?
The ship, the ship!
Isolda's ship!—
Thou must discern it,
must perceive it!
The ship—dost thou see it?—

(*Whilst* KURVENAL, *still hesitating, opposes* TRISTAN, *the Shepherd's pipe is heard without, playing a joyous strain.*)

KURVENAL (*springing joyously up*).
O rapture! Transport!

(*He rushes to the watch-tower and looks out.*)

Ha! the ship!
From northward it is nearing.

TRISTAN. So I knew,
so I said!
Yes, she yet lives,
and life to me gives.
How could Isold'
from this world be free,
which only holds
Isolda for me?

KURVENAL (*shouting*). Ahoy! Ahoy!
See her bravely tacking!
How full the canvas is filled!
How she darts! how she flies!

TRISTAN. The pennon? the pennon?

KURVENAL. A flag is floating at mast-head,
joyous and bright.

TRISTAN. Aha! what joy!
Now through the daylight
comes my Isolda.
Isolda, oh come!
See'st thou herself?

KURVENAL. The ship is shut
from me by rocks.

TRISTAN. Behind the reef?
Is there not risk!
Those dangerous breakers
ships have oft shattered.—
Who steereth the helm?

KURVENAL. The steadiest seaman.

TRISTAN. Betrays he me?
Is he Melot's ally?

KURVENAL. Trust him like me.

TRISTAN. A traitor thou, too!—
O caitiff!
Canst thou not see her?

KURVENAL. Not yet.

TRISTAN. Destruction!

KURVENAL. Aha! Halla-halloa I
they clear! they clear!
Safely they clear!
Inside the surf
steers now the ship to the strand.

TRISTAN (*shouting in joy*). Hallo-ho! Kurvenal!
Trustiest friend!
All the wealth I own
to-day I bequeath thee.

KURVENAL. With speed they approach.

TRISTAN. Now dost thou see her?
See'st thou Isolda?

KURVENAL. 'Tis she! she waves!

TRISTAN. O woman divine!

KURVENAL. The ship is a-land!
Isolda.'—ha!—
With but one leap
lightly she springs to land!

TRISTAN. Descend from the watch-tow'r,
indolent gazer!
Away! away
to the shore!
Help her! help my belov'd!

KURVENAL. In a trice she shall come;
Trust in my strong arm!
But thou, Tristan,
hold thee tranquilly here!

(*He hastens off.*)

TRISTAN (*tossing on his couch in feverish excitement*).
O sunlight glowing,
glorious ray!
Ah, joy-bestowing
radiant day!
Boundeth my blood,
boisterous flood!
Infinite gladness!
Rapturous madness!
Can I bear to lie
couched here in quiet?
Away, let me fly
to where hearts run riot!
Tristan the brave,
exulting in strength,
has torn himself
from death at length.

(*He raises himself erect.*)

All wounded and bleeding
Sir Morold I defeated;
all bleeding and wounded
Isolda now shall be greeted.

(*He tears the bandage from his wound.*)

Ha, ha, my blood!
Merrily flows it.

(*He springs from his bed and staggers forward.*)

She who can help
my wound and close it,
she comes in her pride,
she comes to my aid.
Be space defied:
let the universe fade!

(*He reels to the centre of the stage.*)

ISOLDA'S VOICE (*without*).
Tristan! Tristan! Belovéd!

TRISTAN (*in frantic excitement*).
What! hails me the light?
The torchlight—ha!—
The torch is extinct!
I come! I come!

SCENE II.

[ISOLDA *hastens breathlessly in.* TRISTAN, *delirious with excitement, staggers wildly towards her. They meet in the centre of the stage; she receives him in her arms, where he sinks slowly to the ground.*]

ISOLDA. Tristan! Ah!

TRISTAN (*turning, his dying eyes on* ISOLDA). Isolda!—

(*He dies.*)

ISOLDA. 'Tis I, 'tis I—
dearly belov'd!
Wake, and once more
hark to my voice!
Isolda calls.
Isolda comes,
with Tristan true to perish.—

Speak unto me!
But for one moment,
only one moment
open thine eyes!
Such weary days
I waited and longed,
that one single hour
I with thee might awaken.
Betrayed am I then?
Deprived by Tristan
of this our solitary,
swiftly fleeting,
final earthly joy?—
His wound, though—where?
Can I not heal it?
The rapture of night
O let us feel it?
Not of thy wounds,
not of thy wounds must thou expire!
Together, at least,
let fade life's enfeebled fire!—
How lifeless his look!—
still his heart!—
Dared he to deal me
Buch a smart?
Stayed is his breathing's
gentle tide!
Must I be wailing
at his side,
who, in rapture coming to seek him,
fearless sailed o'er the sea?
Too late, too late!
Desperate man!
Casting on me
this cruelest ban!
Comes no relief
for my load of grief?
Silent art keeping
while I am weeping?
But once more, ah!
But once again!—
Tristan!—ha!
he wakens—hark!

Beloved—
—dark!

(She sinks down senseless upon his body.)

SCENE III.

[KURVENAL, *who reëntered close behind* ISOLDA, *has remained by the entrance speechless and petrified, gazing motionless on* TRISTAN. *From below is now heard the dull murmur of voices and the clash of weapons. The Shepherd clambers over the wall.*]

SHEPHERD *(coming hastily and softly to* KURVENAL*)*.
Kurvenal! Hear!
Another ship!

(KURVENAL *starts up in haste and looks over the rampart, whilst the Shepherd stands apart, gazing in consternation on* TRISTAN *and* ISOLDA.)

KURVENAL. Fiends and furies!

(In a burst of anger.)

All are at hand!
Melot and Mark
I see on the strand,—
Weapons and missiles!—
Guard we the gate!

(He hastens with the Shepherd to the gate, which they both try quickly to barricade.)

THE STEERSMAN *(rushing in)*.
Mark and his men
have set on us:
defence is vain!
We're overpowered.

KURVENAL. Stand to and help!—
While lasts my life
I'll let no foe enter here!

BRANGÆNA'S VOICE *(without, calling from below)*.
Isolda! Mistress!

KURVENAL. Brangæna's voice! *(Falling down.)*
What want you here?

BRANGÆNA. Open, Kurvenal!
Where is Isolda?

KURVENAL. With foes do you come?
Woe to you, false one!

MELOT'S VOICE (*without*). Stand back, thou fool!
Bar not the way!

KURVENAL (*laughing savagely*). Hurrah for the day
on which I confront thee!

(MELOT, *with armed men, appears under the gateway.* KURVENAL *falls on him and cuts him down.*)

Die, damnable wretch!

SCENE IV.

MELOT. Woe's me!—Tristan! (*He dies.*)

BRANGÆNA (*still without*). Kurvenal! Madman!
O hear—thou mistakest!

KURVENAL. Treacherous maid! (*To his men.*)
Come! Follow me!
Force them below! (*They fight.*)

MARK (*without*). Hold, thou frantic man!
Lost are thy senses?

KURVENAL. Here ravages Death!
Nought else, O king,
is here to be holden!
If you would earn it, come on!

(*He sets upon* MARK *and his followers.*)

MARK. Away, rash maniac!

BRANGÆNA (*has climbed over the wall at the side and hastens in the front*).
Isolda! lady!
Joy and life!—
What sight's here—ha!
Liv'st thou, Isolda! (*She goes to* ISOLDA'S *aid.*)

MARK (*who with his followers has driven* KURVENAL *and his men back from the gate and forced his way in*). O wild mistake! Tristan, where art thou?

KURVENAL (*desperately wounded, totters before* MARK *to the front*).
He lieth—there—
here, where I lie too.—

(*Sinks down at* TRISTAN'S *feet.*)

MARK. Tristan! Tristan!
Isolda! Woe!

KURVENAL (*trying to grasp* TRISTAN'S *hand*).
Tristan! true lord!
Chide me not
that I try to follow thee! (*He dies.*)

MARK. Dead together!—
All are dead!
My hero Tristan!
truest of friends,
must thou again
be to thy king a traitor?
Now, when he comes
another proof of love to give thee!
Awaken! awaken.
O hear my lamentation,
thou faithless, faithful friend!

(*Kneels down sobbing over the bodies.*)

BRANGÆNA (*who has revived* ISOLDA *in her arms*).
She wakes! she lives!
Isolda, hear!
Hear me, mistress beloved!
Tidings of joy
I have to tell thee:
O list to thy Brangæna!
My thoughtless fault I have atoned;
after thy flight
I forthwith went to the king:
the love potion's secret
he scarce had learned
when with sedulous haste
he put to sea,
that he might find thee,
nobly renounce thee
and give thee up to thy love.

MARK. O why, Isolda,
Why this to me?
When clearly was disclosed
what before I could fathom not,
what joy was mine to find
my friend was free from fault!

In haste to wed
thee to my hero
with flying sails
I followed thy track:
but howe'er can
happiness
o'ertake the swift course of woe?
More food for Death did I make:
more wrong grew in mistake.

BRANGÆNA. Dost thou not hear?
Isolda! Lady!
O try to believe the truth!

ISOLDA (*unconscious of all around her, turning her eyes with, rising inspiration on* TRISTAN'S *body*).
Mild and softly
he is smiling;
how his eyelids sweetly open!
See, oh comrades,
see you not
how he beameth
ever brighter—
how he rises
ever radiant
steeped in starlight,
borne above?
See you not
how his heart
with lion zest,
calmly happy
beats in his breast?
From his lips
in heavenly rest
sweetest breath
he softly sends.
Harken, friends!
Hear and feel ye not?
Is it I
alone am hearing
strains so tender
and endearing?
Passion swelling,
all things telling,

gently bounding,
from him sounding,
in me pushes,
upward rushes
trumpet tone
that round me gushes.
Brighter growing,
o'er me flowing,
are these breezes
airy pillows?
Are they balmy
beauteous billows?
How they rise
and gleam and glisten!
Shall I breathe them?
Shall I listen?
Shall I sip them,
dive within them,
to my panting
breathing win them?
In the breezes around,
in the harmony sound
in the world's driving
whirlwind be drown'd—
and, sinking,
be drinking—
in a kiss,
highest bliss!

(ISOLDA *sinks, as if transfigured, in* BRANGÆNA'S *arms upon* TRISTAN'S *body. Profound emotion and grief of the bystanders.* MARK *invokes a blessing on the dead. Curtain.*)

Milton Keynes UK
Ingram Content Group UK Ltd.
UKHW040839141024
449705UK00006B/384